DIVIDER OF THE COMMON WEALTH

How The Rich Devoured The World

Christopher P. Hill

Although the author and publisher have made every effort to ensure that the information in this book was correct at press time, the author and publisher do not assume and hereby disclaim any liability to any party for any loss, damage, or disruption caused by errors or omissions, whether such errors or omissions result from negligence, accident or any other cause. This publication is solely for personal growth and is sold with the understanding that neither the author nor publisher is engaged in presenting professional advice.

This book is copyright © 2022 by Christopher P. Hill with all rights reserved.

No part of this book may be reproduced or transmitted in any form whatsoever, electronic or mechanical including photocopying, recording, or by any informational storage or retrieval system without expressed written, dated, and signed permission from the author.

TABLE OF CONTENTS

Chapter 1 4
Disagreement Of Economic Policies And Poverty

Chapter 2 30
Growth For The Poor

Chapter 3 60
Considering Averages

Chapter 4 88
Growth, Distribution And Poverty Reduction

Chapter 5 112
Geographic Profile Of Profit: Evidence From Three Developing Countries

Chapter 1

Disagreement Of Economic Policies And Poverty

This brief period marked the end of history. The late 1990s crushed any aspirations that there would be a broad-based agreement on economic policy for growth, fairness, and the eradication of poverty that had been raised in the early 1990s. That was made possible by the East Asian crisis and the Seattle fiasco. In 2000, the World Bank's governors, whose goal is to end poverty, could only meet under police protection due to protests by people who thought the organization and the policies it supports are to blame for poverty.

The Prague, Seattle, and Washington, DC protests are only one manifestation of a spectrum of dissent that also includes fervent discussion in the pages of major newspapers, fervent support from religious groups, and the polite back and forth of scholarly conversation. I've participated in a protracted consultation process on methods to reduce poverty over the last two years. The consultation contacted the majority of interested parties in academia, policy, and campaigning communities.

It covered government ministries in the North and the South, northern aid organizations, academic analysts in rich and poor countries, northern and southern advocacy non-governmental organizations (NGOs), and NGOs with ground-level operations working with the poor. It also covered the international financial institutions (IFIs) and the countless UN specialized agencies. There were several meetings, traditional paper comments, a worldwide internet consultation, and more.

The deliberate effort to directly extract the "voices of the impoverished" via participatory evaluations was a particularly beneficial exercise. This chapter offers an examination of the major points of contention in both these discussions and among individuals who are generally interested in reducing poverty. First of all, it should be emphasized that there is a great deal of unanimity now where there would not have been two decades ago. The first step in any discussion of differences must be to identify these points of agreement. However, it is evident that there are significant gaps in economic planning, distribution, and poverty. These conflicts manifested themselves during the discussions, sometimes civilly but occasionally in furious written and verbal dialogue that foreshadowed future street fights.

How can individuals with apparently similar aims disagree so much on how to get there, and how can seemingly identical objective reality be viewed so differently? is a subject the chapter attempts to address. Of course, the straightforward response—which the protagonists themselves often give—is to cast doubt on the intentions or critical thinking skills of people with whom one disagrees. Never very far below the surface is the implication that "the others" are either not really concerned in combating poverty (quite the reverse, in reality), or that they make simple factual or interpretive mistakes. Here, it is said, at least part of the dispute may be explained by contrasting viewpoints and conceptual frameworks.

It is more beneficial to promote discourse than conflict when disputes are seen in this way rather than in terms of motivations or intellect. The goal of this chapter is to explain some of the fundamental causes of significant differences in economic policy, distribution, and poverty and to do so in an analytical framework as opposed to a rhetorical one. But first, a bit more regarding arguments about what and disagreements between whom is necessary.

The timing and sequencing of fiscal adjustment, monetary and interest rate policy, exchange rate regimes, trade and openness, internal and external financial liberalization, including the deregulation of capital flows, the scope, and tactics of large-scale privatization of state-owned enterprises, etc., are all major points of contention. Trade and openness may be the quintessential, illustrative subject that engenders the greatest conflicts and the worst language. Any effort at categorization and classification runs the danger of undermining a reality that is intricate and deeply nuanced. However, the grouping that follows covers the main aspects of policy differences and would be familiar to most people. One team, let's call them Group A, may be referred to as the "financial ministry." Those who worked in the finance ministries of the North and the South would undoubtedly be included in this category. It would also include many

The IFIs and the regional multilateral banks employ economic analysts, managers of economic policy, and operational managers. The financial press, especially in the North but also in the South, would be a crucial component. Last but not least, one would include many academic economists educated in the Anglo-Saxon tradition, albeit not all. Another group, let's call them Group B, may be referred to as "civil society." Analysts and advocates from the broad spectrum of advocacy and operational NGOs would undoubtedly be included in this category. Additionally, there would be personnel working for humanitarian ministries in the North and social sector ministries in the South, as well as for some of the UN's specialized organizations. Non-economist scholars would typically belong to this category.

To reiterate, any such categorization would inevitably be an overly simplistic portrayal of reality. Although using the terms "Group A" and "Group B" makes things simpler, it's preferable to think of A and B as inclinations rather than as clearly defined groups of people. There are undoubtedly IFI employees who are not "finance ministry types," just as there are academic economists with Anglo-Saxon backgrounds who would, for instance, express significant reservations about capital account reform.

The conflict between the finance ministry and civil society inclinations often takes place in the UN specialized agencies and northern assistance organizations. It is made clear in the next section that certain NGO opinions on particular policies would be accepted in finance ministries and vice versa. Despite this, the suggested categorization provides a clear enough and recognizable characterization of differences to assist in our understanding of the nature of conflicts.

People in Group A have a tendency to think that the greatest way to reduce poverty is to make more fast adjustments to fiscal imbalances, quickly reduce inflation and external deficits, and employ high-interest rates to accomplish these goals. Sector liberalization, relaxation of capital restrictions, quick and significant openness of an economy to trade and foreign direct investment, and possibly the biggest commonality among them is the rapid and massive privatization of state-owned firms. Group B personalities often take the opposing stance on each of these problems.

The actual question at hand is, "Why?" Why do these two groups differ so sharply on fundamental economic policy issues? This chapter's main argument is that judgments of economic policy, distribution, and poverty are often characterized by disparities in viewpoint and framework on three major factors: aggregate, time horizon, and market structure. First, compared to Group B, Group A has a tendency to perceive the effects of economic policy in considerably more aggregative terms.

Second, compared to Group A's normal "medium-term" view, Group B is more concerned with the effects across a time horizon that is both considerably shorter and much longer. Third, Group A naturally thinks of a world in which market structure is characterized by pockets of market power, and economic policy feeds through this non-competitive structure to the consequences for the poor. In contrast, Group B naturally thinks of a world in which market structure is non-competitive.

The main goal of this chapter is to elaborate on Aggregation, Time Horizon, and Market Structure in order to provide a framework for comprehending profound debates about distribution, poverty, and economic policy. But let's first discuss areas of agreement rather than focusing on areas of conflict. There is no denying that there is now widespread consensus that when determining poverty and the effects of economic policy, education and health outcomes should be compared to income. Since this has become so ordinary, it is easy to forget that 25 years ago, the World Bank engaged in significant intellectual and political struggles about how to redefine development and the fight against poverty. Perhaps today's fresh ideas on how to conceptualize poverty, such as the idea that participation and empowerment should be valued equally alongside money, education, and health, will also serve as tomorrow's pillars.

The discussions also demonstrated broad consensus—at least at a certain degree of generality—on the contribution of global public goods to the welfare of the underprivileged. It was widely acknowledged that public involvement is required in these regions, regardless of how it was couched—as cross-border spillovers of environmental externalities or financial instability, or as the key function of basic research into tropical agriculture and tropical illnesses. Most people had an innate understanding of this issue's growing relevance. This positive situation might very well be a result of the fact that this is a relatively recent policy problem; yet, as we get into the divisions, specifics, will increase. So, for instance, although the notion of a vaccine purchase fund to bridge the gap between the expenses of fundamental research and the buying capacity of the poorest nations was generally supported, there was some disagreement.

There was already considerable opposition to the idea that such monies were unjustified corporate subsidies and should instead be used to provide businesses with the medications they already had at cost-effective pricing. The classic "markets vs state" issue is a third area where there is a startling degree of consensus, or more precisely, not as much disagreement as there was 20 or even 10 years ago. On this, there has undoubtedly been some convergence.

The opinions of NGOs with genuine on-the-ground operations who interact directly with the impoverished were particularly noteworthy. These groups tended to be highly practical throughout the dialogues. They were never concerned with philosophies that favored the state over the market or the other way around; rather, they were concerned with what helped raise the quality of life for the people they were trying to aid. Think about the initiatives and guiding principles of SEWA, the Self Employed Women's Association, which works in Gujarat State, India.

Ahmedabad has a long history of organizing textile workers, and SEWA arose out of it and used those skills to coordinate women in the unorganized sector. From an urban foundation, it has now grown to include organizing in rural regions. SEWA's grassroots initiatives and national lobbying activities are examples of pragmatism that avoids taking a stand on the "state versus market" issue. Because various forms of trade liberalization improve demand for their members' products and labor, they have backed them.

However, they have fought against various forms of trade liberalization when they negatively impacted, for instance, the job and income of the spouses, brothers, and fathers of their members. They are ardent proponents of loosening the Gujarat State Forestry Commission's grip on the members' means of subsistence. However, they are opposed to pharmaceutical sector deregulation due to the disastrous effects on the cost of essential medications, and they are in favor of tighter control in export processing zones to guarantee that labor standards are fulfilled.

Is SEWA more pro-market or pro-state? It is challenging to say. It is evident that SEWA supports the underprivileged. In fact, one of their most well-known booklets is called "Liberalizing for the Poor." Pragmatism gives place to more defined a priori viewpoints on state and markets the more one travels away from ground-level activities and the further one moves to advocacy organizations of any shade. Even still, the gaps are not as wide as they were at the Cold War's height or at the height of post-Cold War triumphalism, which signaled the "end of history." The fundamental issues at the turn of the century have to do with finding the ideal ratio between the market and the government, as well as how things function in practice. Along with this narrowing of the gap between markets and the state, there is general agreement on the critical role that institutions play in governing government, regulating markets, defining how households engage in the marketplace, and ultimately determining the results for the poor.

The importance of institutions like the police and the courts to the reality of poor people's lives was one of the Voices of the Poor exercise's most stunning discoveries. In the meetings, it was also determined that institutions have a macro-level role in influencing the investment environment. Again, this was at a certain degree of generality, of course. Divisions tended to surface when in-depth talks began, particularly when they affected economic policy. In contrast with the differences that are the subject of this chapter, there is thus widespread unanimity in certain areas and at a particular level of discourse. But the very agreements themselves highlight the unresolved issues.

Because the struggle is now sharply concentrated on a decreasing number of subjects, it almost seems like the conflict is more severe. There is a distinct feeling of individuals talking past one another in the contemporary conversation on economic policy, distribution, and poverty even when faced with what seems to be the same objective fact, each side is equally sure that it is right and has the truth. How is it possible? When discussing outcomes or the effects of various economic policy initiatives, different persons naturally function at different levels of aggregation, which is one important consideration.

This goes beyond the conventional way that this split is depicted, which simply compares GDP to poverty or other distribution measures. Many individuals in Group A now use poverty measurements, which, for instance, determine the percentage of people in a nation who earn or spend below a key threshold.

The renowned poverty line of $1 per person per day is the benchmark that is most often utilized. Even with a metric like this, the two groups' views on the effects of poverty are significantly different. Some of the distinctions are plain to see, while others are less so. The following personal story serves as an example of the response that many analysts in Group A encounter when they offer their formal analyses of poverty to larger audiences.

In the 1980s and early 1990s, I conducted extensive academic research on the Ghana Living Standards Survey (GLSS), and in 1992 I found myself in charge of the World Bank's field office in Ghana. Numerous analysts' analyses of GLSS data revealed that between 1987 and 1991, Ghana's incidence of poverty—defined as above but with a local poverty line—fell. There was a three to four percentage point reduction throughout these four years, albeit the precise amount varied based on the precise computations. Although it was pathetically little, this was excellent by African standards.

The study given contained all the essential modifications and changes to get over the drawbacks of this kind of data, much as the best practice in the field. In order to get at the poverty measure, for instance, a great deal of work was put into adjusting for regional pricing fluctuations, creating imputations for homes, correcting for family size, etc. However, relatively few individuals in Ghana accepted the analysis when it was given to them.

There was an astounding level of skepticism among university scholars, international and local NGOs, labor unions, and rotary clubs. This is a frequent response to research that reveals a decline in poverty, at least in Africa. Group A analysts' typical responses to such skepticism run the range from claims that the critics are members of special interest organizations, that individuals just do not grasp the statistical analysis in its entirety, that certain people would never recognize that they are better off, etc. However, it is wise to take into account that there may be valid explanations for this reaction that are reasonable even within the conventional framework of research based on household surveys before rejecting skepticism in this manner. The assertion that poverty has decreased in Ghana, for instance, may be called into doubt for at least three different reasons.

Analysts of household surveys are familiar with the first of these. The income expenditure-based assessment of well-being has significantly advanced over time. For instance, output for domestic consumption is now usually included, the capture of regional price variation is improving, and imputing use value to homes is also becoming normal. The value of public services, however, is one thing that these criteria do not adequately or at all quantify.

There are other modules in similar surveys that include questions on infrastructure, health, education, and other topics, but due to conceptual and data challenges, they are seldom, if ever, incorporated into the income-expenditure measure of well-being. The headline poverty ratios are derived using this income-expenditure metric.

Therefore, it is quite feasible for public services to significantly deteriorate while yet having no impact on the income-expenditure-based estimates of poverty incidence. If a woman's bus service from her village to her sister's village is canceled, it won't be accounted for in these measurements. If the urban slum's health post runs out of medication, it won't be there. It won't display if the primary school textbooks are missing or if the instructor is absent. However, those with operations and staff on the ground will notice these. The assertion that poverty has decreased will sound hollow to them as well as to the poor.

All of this is not meant to imply that calculating income-expenditure poverty estimates based on nationally representative household surveys is not relevant. It simply means that concentrating just on them leaves out disaggregated material that others may assist fill in and that affects their perceptions and judgments. The second cause of the discrepancy between Group A's poverty measurements, which are based on household surveys, and Group B's views of poverty is regional or group disaggregation. Even if we assume that income-expenditure-based indicators accurately reflect wellbeing, a nationwide decline in the incidence of poverty often consists of significant moves in the other direction. For instance, in Ghana, between 1987 and 1991, an increase in urban areas coincided with a decrease in national poverty. Between 1990 and 1994, Mexico had a countrywide decline in poverty; yet, certain rural areas saw an increase.

It's critical to understand that we're not discussing a few unfortunate households getting by. The overall regional poverty index rose. While it is obvious to celebrate the reduction in the national poverty index and the declines in the areas that are responsible for it, concentrating just on the overall picture runs the risk of omitting the rising poverty in Accra, the capital of Ghana, or in the Mexican state of Chiapas. It is cold consolation to be told, "but national poverty has gone down," for an NGO working with street children in Accra or for a municipal government dealing with rising poverty among indigenous peoples in Chiapas. Similar arguments may be made for gender-based disaggregation and other classifications based on race and ethnicity. It should be obvious that in the disconnect described above, neither point of view is "wrong." The same objective truth is being viewed and exaggerated in many ways.

It is accurate to say that key groups have suffered while the prevalence of poverty as a whole has decreased. The issue is that neither side makes an effort to grasp the other side's viewpoint, instead choosing to defend their own in ever-sharper terms. While Group B analysts and activists get more annoyed and alienated from a language that contradicts the reality they are familiar with, Group A analysts just keep reiterating that poverty has decreased and do not make any accommodations to the intricate group-specific patterns.

Now consider a third disconnect related to aggregation that is sometimes overlooked. The primary measure of poverty used by Group A analysts is the incidence of poverty, which is the proportion of the population that lives in poverty. Let's imagine that each individual receives $1 every day. These are the ideas they automatically gravitate toward. For instance, donor organizations generally agree that the main international development goal is to halve the prevalence of poverty by 2015. But in Group B, analysts, advocates, and particularly operational types automatically use the absolute number of impoverished as the criteria.

The possibility of disconnecting ought to be obvious. In Ghana, for instance, the incidence of poverty decreased by about one percentage point per year between 1987 and 1991, but the overall population increased by almost twice that amount. As a result, even using the traditional income expenditure-based measure, the absolute number of poor increased noticeably.

Reconsider the local NGO that conducts activities on the ground. Those who work in these groups would argue, very reasonably from their viewpoint, that poverty has increased if more people are visiting soup meals, more homeless indigents need refuge, and more street children are appearing. They don't find it very important that poverty rates have decreased, and being told this constantly and adamantly will inevitably make it harder to communicate and have a meaningful conversation. This is also apparent on a worldwide scale.

According to data from the World Bank, throughout the 1990s, the absolute number of the poor basically remained steady at 1.2. billion. Due to an increase in the global population, poverty rates have decreased. Has the world's poverty decreased or remained the same? During the meetings, the question, "How can you argue economic expansion benefits the poor?" was often raised. Look, despite all this expansion in the 1990s, there were still a ton of people living in poverty.

Putting the growth problem aside, it is simple to understand how communication might be stymied when various groups interpret poverty in different ways. Clarity and understanding would be a good place to start in this situation, but even it would not be enough to make a difference since it is still unclear whether the criterion should be the incidence of poverty or the sheer number of poor people. Therefore, at least part of the disconnect one perceives may be explained by the automatic use of various levels of aggregation in presenting and analyzing the distributional and poverty effects of economic policy.

Each of the economic policies under discussion, such as the effects of changing trade policy on distribution and poverty, would be subject to the arguments and categorizations mentioned above. Understanding these differences is the first step in having a more fruitful conversation with those who have a much more finely disaggregated view of the results of economic policy and those who primarily rely on national poverty incidence measures derived from household surveys to assess the evolution of poverty. Sadly, at this time, there is polarization due to the lack of mutual understanding, with Group A frequently withdrawing into the formal technical bunker and simply repeating their findings without attempting to understand what Group B is trying to say, and Group B dismissing Group A analysis as either out of touch with reality or, worse yet, actively manipulated to get certain answers.

Moving ahead, we must overcome the aggregation gap since none of these stances is healthy. Others have what they perceive to be a far greater time horizon than ten years. This section includes environmental organizations that have a religious stance on resource management. They believe that the 50- or 100-year view is crucial. Given the limitations of the earth's carrying capacity, they do not see how economic development can be continued, and they recognize both the short- and long-term detrimental effects of resource depletion.

A key implication of this line of reasoning is that, to reduce global poverty, redistribution, whether implicit or explicit, from affluent to poor nations will have to take the place of economic development. They make reference to the doomsday predictions made by the Club of Rome in the 1970s and make note of the fact that none of them came to pass. The solution is to correct these distortions rather than forcefully suppressing investment and development, even if there are undoubtedly certain market distortions that result in an inefficiently high degree of resource depletion and cross-border spillover effects that cause their coordination issues.

In any case, they do not believe that asking the wealthy nations to implement significant redistribution in favor of the poor nations is a politically viable option over the next five to ten years. Instead, they have a strong belief that technological advancement will save the day over the next fifty or one hundred years, as it has in the past. Therefore, Group A was fighting against both shorter-term and longer-term viewpoints throughout the talks. But the actual issue is that, more often than not, it was unclear whether the intricacies of trade policy were at fault or this disparity in viewpoint.

The discrepancy was caused by privatization policies, for example, or something else. Clarity is a beginning, not a solution.

Chapter 2

Growth For The Poor

Despite the East Asian financial crisis, the global economy developed well throughout the 1990s. Over how much the poor gain from this prosperity, however, there is a lot of disagreement. The two aforementioned quotations serve as an example of this argument's extremes. On one end of the spectrum, there are those who contend that the sharp increases in inequality that come along with growth completely negate or even negate the potential advantages of economic growth for the poor.

The claim that liberal economic policies, such as monetary and fiscal stability and free markets, boost the earnings of the poor and everyone else in society proportionally is at the opposite extreme of the spectrum. It is remarkable how little rigorous cross-country empirical information is available on the degree to which the poorest members of society gain from economic development given the raging public discussion on this topic and its apparent policy implications. Using a large sample of developed and developing nations spanning the last four decades, we empirically examine the relationship between growth in average incomes of the poor and growth in overall incomes in this chapter.

The poor are defined as those in the bottom fifth of the income distribution of a country. This method is equivalent to examining how a specific measure of income inequality—the first quintile share—varies with average incomes because average incomes of the poor are proportional to the share of income accruing to the poorest quintile times average income.

We are unable to disprove the null hypothesis that the income share of the top quintile does not consistently fluctuate with average earnings across a large sample of nations covering the previous four decades. In other words, the null hypothesis that the incomes of the poor rise in proportion to average incomes cannot be rejected. The fact that both variables are logarithmically calculated suggests that, on average, the poor's earnings climb proportionally to average incomes. Using 285 country-year observations with at least two observations on poor incomes per country that are separated by at least five years, we plot the average annual growth in poor incomes (on the vertical axis) against the average annual growth in average incomes (on the horizontal axis) in the bottom panel.

Ninety-two nations make up the sample, and each had three growth episodes on average. Once again, there is a significant, positive, linear association with a slope of 1.19 between these two variables. The null hypothesis that the slope of this relationship is equal to one cannot be ruled out in the majority of the formal statistical tests that follow. These regressions show that within nations, the earnings of the poor generally increase in line with average incomes.

This is comparable to noting that average earnings and the proportion of income going to the bottom fifth of the income distribution do not correlate predictably. In the sections that follow, we look more closely at this fundamental finding and discover that it is resilient to accounting for potential reverse causation from the earnings of the poor to average incomes and holds across locations, periods, growth rates, and income levels. We next investigate whether policies and institutions that increase average incomes have systematic effects on the share of income going to the poorest quintile, which could magnify or cancel out their effects on the incomes of the poor.

This is because there is a strong correlation between the incomes of the poor and average incomes. We concentrate our efforts on a group of institutions and policies whose significance for average earnings has been noted in the extensive cross-national empirical literature on economic growth. These include being open to international commerce, having a stable macroeconomic environment, having a small but functional government, developing the financial sector, and having strong property rights and the rule of law.

There is no evidence to suggest that these institutions and policies affect the percentage of income going to the lowest quintile systematically. There are just two exceptions: there is some shaky evidence that a smaller government and stabilization from high inflation favor the poor by increasing the percentage of income going to the lowest quintile. These results suggest that policies and institutions that promote development often help the poor—as well as everyone else in society—equitably.

We further demonstrate that, compared to their influence on overall economic development, such factors often have little distributional consequences. Next, we look more closely at the widely held belief that growing economic interdependence among nations is linked to rising national inequality. We first take a look at a variety of indicators of global openness, including trade volumes, tariffs, WTO membership, and the existence of capital restrictions, and we examine if any of these factors has a consistent impact on the proportion of income that goes to the lowest sections of society. We find no evidence to support this claim, and this finding remains true even when we allow the impacts of openness measures to be influenced by variations in factor endowments and levels of development, as expected by the factor proportions theory of international commerce. As a result, we are likewise unable to reject the null hypothesis that increasing economic integration generally helps society's most vulnerable members equally.

Making growth even more "pro-poor" has received a lot of attention recently in the development world. We interpret this emphasis on "pro-poor" growth as a call for some other policy interventions that raise the share of income captured by the poorest in society given our evidence that neither growth nor growth-enhancing policies tend to be systematically associated with changes in the share of income accruing to the poorest fifth of societies.

We empirically investigate the impact of four such possible factors—primary educational attainment, public health and education expenditure, labor productivity in agriculture compared to the rest of the economy, and formal democratic institutions—on the income share of the poorest. We were unable to find any proof that these variables consistently increase the percentage of income earned by the poorest in our large cross-country sample, despite the likelihood that they do so in certain nations and situations. In summary, we find no evidence that the income share of the lowest quintile is strongly correlated with either average incomes or a broad range of policy and other factors.

As a result, we are unable to reject the null hypothesis that impoverished people's earnings generally increase in line with average incomes. Of course, this does not imply that disregarding the distributional implications of policies and assuming that growth alone would better the situation of society's weakest citizens. We utilize current cross-country data on income distribution, which has significant measurement error, which we go into more depth about below. We thus cannot rule out the likelihood that this measurement error is the only cause of our inability to identify systematic impacts of average incomes and policy on the income share of the lowest quintile.

Additionally, we cannot completely rule out the possibility that there are intricate relationships between inequality and growth that are not reflected in our straightforward empirical models and result in negligible changes in the former that are unrelated to the latter. We can, however, draw the following conclusion: Effective poverty reduction strategies are likely to focus on policies that increase average incomes, and existing cross-country evidence, including our own, offers disappointingly little guidance as to what combination of growth-oriented policies might particularly benefit the most vulnerable members of society.

Our research draws on and adds to two distinct streams of inequality and growth literature. Our fundamental conclusion, which holds that increases in inequality and income are independent, is in line with those of other earlier researchers, notably *Deininger and Squire (1996), Chen and Ravallion (1997),* and *Easterly (1999),* who have found the same pattern in smaller samples of nations. By taking into account a significantly larger sample of nations and using more sophisticated econometric techniques, we expand on this literature by accounting for the possibility that income levels are endogenous to inequality, as suggested by the extensive theoretical and empirical literature on the effects of inequality on growth.

Our findings are also connected to the sparse but expanding body of research on the factors that influence how indices of income inequality vary between countries and across time. First off, we lack corresponding data on mean income from the same source for many of the country-year observations for which we have information on income distribution.

Second, using per capita GDP makes it easier for us to compare our findings to the vast body of literature on income distribution and growth, which frequently employs the same methodology. We treat the differences between per capita GDP and household income on the one hand, and per capita GDP on the other, as classical measurement error because there is no evidence of a systematic correlation between these variables, as will be covered in more detail below.

When calculating the income of the poor, which we define as the poorest 20% of the population, we use two different methods. From nationally representative household surveys for 796 country year observations spanning 137 countries, we can gather data on the percentage of income going to the poorest quintile. When calculating the mean income for these observations, we divide the percentage of income generated by the lowest quintile times mean income by 0.2.

We have information on the Gini coefficient but not the first quintile share for an additional 158 country year data. Assuming a lognormal income distribution for these data, the percentage of income going to the lowest quintile is calculated as the 20th percentile of this distribution. We have collected information on income distribution from four distinct sources. The UNU/WIDER World Income Inequality Database, which is a significant expansion of the income distribution data set created by Deininger and Squire, serves as our main source (1996). This source yields a total of 706 observations for our national year.

Additionally, we get 97 observations that were initially part of the sample and were deemed to be of "good quality" by *Deininger and Squire (1996)* but are absent from the UNU/WIDER data collection. Our third data source is *Chen and Ravallion (2000)*, who employ 265 household surveys from 83 developing nations to create metrics of income distribution and poverty. We only acquire an extra 118 current observations from this source since many of the data from this and prior Chen-Ravallion compilations are directly reported in the Deininger-Squire and UNU/WIDER compilations. Finally, we supplement our data set with 32 observations, mostly from industrialized nations, that are reported in Lundberg and Squire but are not included in the aforementioned three sources (2000). In all, 953 observations from 137 different nations are included in this sample, which spans the years 1950–1999.

To our knowledge, this is the biggest data collection utilized to examine the connection between income disparity, growth, and income inequality. While continuous time series of yearly data on income distribution are available for certain nations over extended periods, most countries only have access to one or a small number of observations, with a median of four observations per country.

We filter the data in the manner described below because medium- to long-term growth is what we are interested in, and we do not want the sample to be dominated by nations whose income distribution statistics just so happen to be more plentiful. We start with the first observation that is available for each country, move forward in time until we reach the next observation, subject to the requirement that at least 5 years elapse between observations, and so on until we have used up all of the information that is currently available for that nation. This leads to an unevenly distributed panel of 418 country-year data on the mean income of the poor, scattered over 137 countries and separated by at least 5 years.

In this smaller sample, the median number of observations per nation is three. In order to take into account within-country growth in mean incomes of the poor over periods of at least five years, we further restrict the sample in our econometric estimation to the set of 285 observations covering 92 countries for which at least two spaced observations on such income are available. These periods typically last six years on average.

The sample is significantly smaller when we take into account the impact of additional control variables, and it varies among specifications based on the available data. It is commonly recognized that comparing statistics on income distribution across nations presents significant challenges. The scope of the survey (national vs subnational), the welfare indicator (income versus consumption), the way in which income is measured (gross versus net), and the unit of observation vary among countries (individuals versus households). We can only very shakily account for these disparities. Our sample is only comprised of data from nationally representative polls on income distribution.

We know whether the welfare indicator is consumption or income for every survey, and for most of them, we also know whether the income indicator is gross or net of taxes and transfers. For the majority of our observations, we lack information on whether the Lorenz curve relates to the percentage of people or the fraction of households, even though we know whether the receiving unit is an individual or a household.

This final piece of information thus offers little assistance in compensating for methodological variations in measurements of income distribution between nations. As a result, we use the following very basic correction for discernible survey type variations. The top quintile share and the Gini coefficient are both regressed on a constant, a set of geographical dummies, and dummy variables indicating whether the welfare measure is gross income or consumption. Our sample consists of 418 observations that are at least 5 years apart.

To arrive at a set of distribution measures that theoretically correspond to the distribution of income net of taxes and transfers, we first remove the estimated mean difference between these two choices and the excluded group. However, as stated in the introduction, it is evident that there is still a very significant amount of measurement error in these income distribution data, so we cannot completely rule out the possibility that this measurement error is the reason we were unable to identify any significant determinants of the income share of the poorest quintile.

Income estimation

We estimate variations of the following regression of the logarithm of the poor's per capita income (y^p) on the logarithm of the average per capita income (y) plus a set of additional control variables (X) in order to look at how the incomes of the poor fluctuate with overall incomes:

$$y^p_{ct} = a_0 + a_1 \dot{c}\, y_{ct} + a' X_{ct} + \mu_c + \varepsilon_{ct},$$

Furthermore, since the first quintile share's logarithm is almost a linear function of the Gini coefficient in empirical terms, it is virtually equal to a regression of the Gini coefficient times the average income and a set of control variables. The need to instrument for these variables is just as compelling as the need to instrument for income due to challenges with measurement error and omitted variables.

Additionally, it's conceivable that endogenous responses to inequality might occur for at least some of the policy variables. However, for two reasons, we decide not to instrument for the X variables in the following. First and foremost, our sample size is significantly decreased by employing the proper delays of these variables as instruments. Indirect proof that the X factors are not linked with the error terms is provided by the fact that tests of overidentifying constraints pass in the specifications where we instrument for income solely.

Anyhow, we find qualitatively pretty comparable findings in the smaller samples when we instrument, thus for the sake of brevity, we just publish a few of the instrumented results. There are grounds to dispute the straightforward OLS conclusions, as was previously stated. The predicted elasticity rises to 1.19 when we instrument for mean income using mean income growth over the five years before as an instrument.

Although this elasticity is computed with considerably less accuracy, we do not disprove the null hypothesis that 1 = 1. Lagged growth is a very significant predictor of the present level of income in the first-stage regression for the levels equation, which gives us some confidence in the validity of the instrument. When we instrument using lagged levels and growth rates of mean income, we get a point estimate of the elasticity of the poor's income with respect to mean income of 0.98 using OLS and a slightly lesser elasticity of 0.91 using this method. We cannot rule out the null hypothesis that the elasticity is equal to one in the OLS or 2SLS data.

Lagged income and twice-lagged growth are both highly significant predictors of growth in the first-stage regression for the differenced equation (given in the second column of the bottom panel). The differenced equation is also overidentified. We do not, at standard significance levels, reject the null of a well-specified model for the differenced equation alone when we test the validity of the overidentifying limitations.

Although statistically insignificant, the interaction term shows that there is little indication that the percentage of income going to the lowest quintile routinely changes during times of slow development. However, if social safety nets are insufficient, it might still be the case that the same percentage loss in income has a higher effect on the poor, and crises may therefore be more difficult on the poor.

However, this is not because their wages are declining faster than those of other societal groups. The 1997 East Asian financial crisis is a superb example of this broad insight. The income share of the lowest quintile actually climbed somewhat between 1996 and 1999 in Indonesia (from 8.0 to 9.0%), Thailand (from 6.1 to 6.4%), and Korea (from 1996 to 1998), but mainly stayed steady following the crisis. This conclusion implies that a variety of institutions and policies linked to better development will likewise proportionally benefit the poor.

However, it's likely that growth from various sources affects the poor in different ways. In this part, we examine a few of the institutions and policies that the empirical growth lowest quintile has identified as being pro-growth.

We focus on five variables: inflation, which *Fischer (1993)* finds to be detrimental to growth; government consumption, which Easterly and *Rebelo (1993)* find to be detrimental to growth; exports and imports as a percentage of GDP, which *Frankel and Romer (1999)* find to be beneficial to growth; a measure of financial development, which *Levine, Loayza, and Beck (2000)* have shown to have significant causal effects on growth; and a measure of the strength of property rights or rule of law.

The specific measurement comes from Kaufmann, *Kraay, and Zobatón (1999). Knack and Keefer* are only two examples of those who have shown the significance of property rights for progress (1995). Since each of these regressions takes into account mean income, the influence of these factors that affect overall growth is already taken into account. Therefore, any differential influence that this variable has on the income of the poor, or alternatively, on the percentage of income flowing to the poor, is captured by the coefficient on the growth determinant itself. We observe a tiny, unfavorable, and statistically insignificant impact of trade volumes on the income share of the poorest quintile.

The same is true for government consumption as a percentage of GDP and inflation, where greater levels of both are linked, although insignificantly, to lower income shares for the lowest quintile. Point estimates for the coefficients on the rule of law and the measure of financial development show that both of these factors are related to larger income shares in the bottom quintile, but once again, each of these impacts is statistically equivalent to zero.

The coefficients on each measure are comparable to those in the simpler regressions when we combine all five measurements. However, it is presently predicted that government consumption as a percentage of GDP has a negative and considerable impact on the income share of the poorest at the 10% level. Additionally, the impact of inflation is still negative and is only marginally significant at the 10% level.

	Trade volumes		Government consumption/GDP		Inflation rate		Financial development		Rule of law index		All growth variables		All growth variables, instrument	
	Coef	Std. err.	Coef	Std. err.	Coef	Std. err.	Coef	Std. err.	Coef	Std. err.	Coef	Std. err.	Coef	Std. err.
ln(per capita GDP)	1.094***	0.108	1.050***	0.085	1.020***	0.089	0.995***	0.119	0.914***	0.105	1.140***	1.100	1.020***	0.128
(Exports + Imports)/GDP	-0.039	0.088									0.023	0.056	-0.067	0.208
Government consumption/GDP			-0.571	0.419							-0.746	0.386	0.401	1.013
ln(1+inflation)					-0.136	0.103					-0.163	0.107	-0.216***	0.077
Commercial bank assets/Total bank assets							0.032	0.257			-0.209	0.172	0.264	0.282
Rule of law									0.084	0.069	-0.032	0.060	-0.011	0.071
P-Ho: X = 1	0.386		0.555		0.825		0.968		0.412		0.164		0.876	
P-OID	0.257		0.168		0.159		0.350		0.279		0.393		0.716	
T-NO-SC	-0.751		-0.506		-0.261		-0.698		-0.945		-0.762		-0.563	
# Observations	223		237		253		232		268		189		137	

Several factors may contribute to the difference between these findings and ours, including
(i) differences in the measure of inequality (all the previous studies consider the Gini index while we focus on the income share of the poorest quintile, although given the high correlation between the two this factor is least likely to be important);

(ii) differences in the sample of countries (with the exception of the paper by Barro, all of the papers cited above restrict attention to considerably smaller and possibly non-representative samples of countries than the seventy-six countries which appear in our basic openness regression, and in addition the paper by Spilimbergo *et al.* uses all available annual observations on inequality with the result that countries with regular household surveys tend to be heavily overrepresented in the sample of pooled observations);

(iii) differences in the measure of openness (Lundberg and Squire 2000, for example, focus on the Sachs–Warner index of openness which has been criticized for proxying the overall policy environment rather than openness *per se*);

(iv) differences in econometric specification and technique.

It is beyond the purview of this brief section to list all of these elements' contributions to the variations in findings. To make our specification more similar to this other research, a few clear expansions of our fundamental model may be used. First, we take into account a variety of openness metrics, some of which are more in line with those used in the earlier research. By regressing our measure of trade volumes on a trade-weighted measure of distance from trading partners and a measure of country size and using the residuals as an adjusted measure of trade volumes, we first (*like Spilimbergo, Londoo, and Székely 1999; Barro 2000*) purge our measure of trade volumes of the geographical determinants of trade.

Because of their time invariance, these geographic factors will only have an impact on our findings to the extent that they are influenced by cross-country data variation and to the extent that these geographic factors for trade volumes are also correlated with the share of the poorest quintile's income. Second, to more closely compare our findings to those of Lundberg and Squire, we employ the Sachs-Warner index (2000). Finally, we also take into account three additional indicators of openness that the aforementioned authors did not take into account: the proportion of collected import taxes to total imports; membership in the World Trade Organization (or its predecessor, the GATT); and restrictions on international capital movements as reported in the International Monetary Fund's Report on Exchange Arrangements and Exchange Coordination.

This shows that our earlier findings about the absence of a connection between average salaries and the log top quintile share are resistant to the addition of these new control variables. Second, there is absolutely no proof that there is a strong inverse link between the average earnings of the poor and any of these openness indicators. With the exception of one example, we are unable to prove the null hypothesis that, when average incomes are held constant, the relevant openness measure does not substantially correlate with the income share of the lowest quintile. The existence of capital restrictions is substantially (at the 10% level) related to a smaller income share of the lowest quintile, making it the sole indicator that deviates from this general trend.

Overall, nevertheless, we draw the conclusion from this table that there is very little proof that there is a meaningful correlation between the income share of the lowest quintile and a variety of metrics of exposure to the global economy. The only other interesting result in this table has nothing to do with openness or the earnings of the underprivileged. We find some evidence that nations with more arable land per worker have a smaller income share of the lowest quintile in the bottom panel, where we also include arable land per capita and its interaction with openness metrics.

In a cross-section of 49 nations, Leamer et al. (1999) found a substantial correlation between increased inequality and farmland per capita. The lowest fifth of a nation's average earnings often increase or decline at the same pace as average incomes.

This is a result of the strong empirical regularity that, across a broad sample of nations over the last four decades, the percentage of income earned by the bottom fifth does not change consistently with average earnings. This association remains true across locations, economic levels, and both regular and emergency situations. Additionally, we discover that a number of pro-growth macroeconomic policies, such as low inflation, a moderately sized government, sound financial development, adherence to the rule of law, and openness to international trade, increase average incomes with little discernible impact on the income distribution.

This bolsters the idea that a fundamental set of policies, including private property rights, fiscal restraint, macroeconomic stability, and trade openness, raises the income of the poor on par with that of other families in society. It is important to stress that our research does not support a "trickle down" process or sequencing in which benefits first benefit the wealthy and then gradually trickle down to the poor. Contrary to popular belief, private property rights, security, and openness simultaneously create an atmosphere that helps everyone, even impoverished families, enhance their output and income.

However, there is no evidence that formal democratic institutions or significant government investment in social services have a consistent impact on the earnings of the poor. Our results do not indicate that all that is required to better the lives of the poor is growth. Instead, we simply stress that, on average, growth benefits the poor just as much as it helps the rest of society. As a result, typical growth-enhancing measures should be at the core of any successful approach to reducing poverty.

This does not imply, however, that the possible distributional implications of development or the growth-promoting policies should or ought to be disregarded. Our findings do not suggest that the income share of the poorest quintile is static; rather, we are unable to relate changes in this share of income across countries and over time to average incomes or to a variety of proxies for the institutions and policies important for economic growth and poverty reduction.

This might be due to the fact that any influence these measures may have on the income share of the lowest quintile is likely to be negligible in comparison to the very large measurement error present in the extremely faulty income distribution statistics we are compelled to use. It could also be because certain theoretical models show that there are intricate relationships between inequality and growth, which our straightforward empirical models are unable to capture.

In conclusion, the cross-country research currently available, including our own, offers sadly little direction as to what combination of growth-oriented policies would notably assist the most disadvantaged members of society. The poorest members of society gain equally from economic development and the institutions and policies that promote it on average, according to our research.

Chapter 3

Considering Averages

Regarding the extent to which the world's poorest people benefit from the economic development fueled by increasing openness to foreign trade and investment, we seem to hold incompatible perspectives. Based on recent research by *Dollar and Kraay (2002)* that indicated that average earnings of the lowest quintile moved almost one-for-one with average incomes overall, The Economist's article is convinced that such growth is effective in eliminating poverty. Although the Dollar and Kraay results and prior findings in the literature all pointed in the same direction, Oxfam's policy director in response to The Economist story seemed equally certain that growing inequality is stifling the potential advantages to the poor.

However, as this chapter will argue, each of the aforementioned quotations has some truth. These two viewpoints may be easily reconciled, and doing so has significant consequences for development policy. I'll rely largely on evidence from a fresh collection of household-level statistics for developing nations as I evaluate the points in this discussion rigorously.

These statistics are discussed in the section that follows. The section focuses on country-level developments after examining how aggregate distribution in the developing world has changed over the last two decades. The chapter then goes into further depth on how distribution affects outcomes for the poor, both as a barrier to development and as a barrier to growth that reduces poverty.

Household surveys, in which random samples of homes are questioned using a standardized questionnaire, provide data on poverty and inequality. The primary information I will utilize in this article relates to "spells," which are defined as the intervals of time between two subsequent household surveys for a specific nation. One may build 120 such periods, largely in the 1990s, using data from the most recent update of the database used to produce the World Bank's income distribution tabulations (*Chen and Ravallion 2001*). This database includes two or more household surveys throughout time for around fifty developing nations.

In order to minimize glaring discrepancies in previous compilations using secondary sources, the estimates of poverty and inequality metrics were made from primary data (rather than utilizing secondary sources). The same economic wellbeing measure, which was either income or spending per person—and is usually regarded to be the favored indicator—is used to compare any two surveys throughout time.

For income or consumption-in-kind derived from own-farm production, imputed values are included. Each metric is population-weighted (taking account of household size and sample expansion factors). The underlying household surveys are representative of the whole country. There are issues with the data. There are fundamental discrepancies (across countries and over time) in the original household surveys that were the basis of the data on household incomes and expenditures, which is among the concerns concerning the data utilized here. Concerns exist over the appropriate approach to adjust nominal values for changes in the cost of living since the consumer price indices that are now available do not always accurately represent the purchasing habits of the underprivileged.

In addition to these issues, there is a chance that household surveys may understate incomes and expenditure, especially (but probably not solely) by the wealthy, who often choose not to participate, are difficult to contact, or purposefully exaggerate their incomes and spending. There isn't much that can be done to resolve these issues. By utilizing analytical techniques that are less likely to be too sensitive to data flaws, one may nevertheless partially account for the data issues.

The issue of "growth of what?" is equally relevant when considering how growth affects poverty. If the poor are benefiting from the rise in the level of life, that is something we want to know. There are, however, two very different and mostly independent sources of information on a nation's average wellbeing, as determined by families' control over commodities. For this, a common metric is the private consumption expenditure (PCE) per capita from the national accounts (NAS).

On the other hand, the same household surveys that are used to quantify poverty also provide data on average household living standards. Both the levels and the growth rates of these two indicators often differ. Given the variations in coverage, definitions, and methodologies, this is not unexpected. The aforementioned issues with survey data exist.

National accounts, meanwhile, have their own data issues. For instance, PCE is often estimated in the NAS residually, after other domestic production uses and imports at the commodity level have been taken into consideration. Although it is unclear how this might affect NAS consumption, there are issues regarding how accurately production and consumption by unincorporated ('informal sector') firms are tracked in developing nations. Another issue is that, in general, it is impossible to distinguish between the expenditure of families and that of non-profit organizations (such as NGOs, religious organizations, and political parties).

PCE may exaggerate the increase rate in household welfare since non-household sectors that are implicitly included with households in many emerging nations look to be sizable and probably rising. Additionally, there are issues with consistency between the two sources, such as those brought about by a poor match between the survey dates and the NAS's accounting periods. The severity of these data problems varies depending on the geography and the kind of survey. In the 1990s, India stood out as an uncommon situation.

The primary national household survey of consumption expenditures does not represent the growth rates in consumption that we have seen in the national accounts for India in the 1990s (the National Sample Survey). The amount of poverty reduction that we are witnessing in the survey data during this time of economic expansion is inevitably being slowed down by this disparity *(Datt 1999)*. The pace of poverty reduction is also decreasing due to indicators that measured inequality is rising given the rate of growth at the same time *(Ravallion 2000)*. How one reads the statistics for India significantly relies on the cause of the growing disparity between the two consumption data sources.

According to one view, surveys understate total consumption, which leads to the conclusion that poverty is decreasing more quickly than the survey statistics indicate *(Bhalla 2000)*. A different perspective contends that the issue is more likely caused by an underestimating of consumption by the non-poor while acknowledging that the surveys are likely missing a portion of the increases in overall consumption. The second explanation would seem to fit our limited understanding of the issues with under-reporting and non-compliance in consumption and income surveys more closely (see, for example, *Groves and Couper 1998*). The correlation between the divergence and India's growth (over time and across states) is also consistent with an income impact on survey underestimate, which one would anticipate to exist also between families (*Ravallion 2000b*). The poverty indicators will still be accurate if the issue is solely the result of underreporting of consumption by the non-poor, who are nonetheless appropriately weighted in the survey design.

The pace of poverty reduction may, however, be underestimated due to sample weighting issues and miscalculation of poor people's consumption. The tests for bias reported in *Ravallion (2000a)* do not indicate a systematic overall discrepancy between national accounts and survey-based estimates of aggregate consumption if one is willing to discount income (rather than expenditure) surveys for measuring average levels of economic welfare and if one sets aside the (highly problematic) data from the transition economies of Central and Eastern Europe for growth rates. (This is true for all nations together; significant inconsistencies may still be observed for particular nations, in both directions.)

However, it is noteworthy that the elasticity of the survey means to NAS consumption growth is less than 1 overall and for the majority of areas (even though the difference is often not statistically significant). This attenuation bias might very well be the result of a measurement mistake. It follows that the measured elasticities of poverty to growth in the survey mean will be fewer than those predicted by the elasticities of measured poverty to NAS growth. It is a strong contender for evaluating the growth rate since the mean from the surveys is consistent with the information used to generate poverty metrics.

This raises still another issue, namely the possibility of spuriously strong correlations between poverty indicators and the distributional means upon which such measures are based. The surveys' measurement errors, which likely led to an erroneous negative association between measured poverty and measured mean, are evidence that strong econometric techniques were used to analyze the data. Later, examples will be provided.

However, it does not follow that growth increases poor people's earnings "by roughly as much as it increases everyone else's incomes." It is not always true that growth improves the earnings of the poor more than the affluent since the percentage of income flowing to the poor does not, on average, vary with growth. Given the current level of inequality, the income gains from distribution-neutral growth will, of course, benefit the wealthy more than the poor. For instance, in India, the income increase for the wealthiest decile will be about four times more than the gain for the lowest quintile; in Brazil, it will be nineteen times greater.

The empirical findings in the literature, including those of Dollar and Kraay, explicitly imply that, on average, the affluent will tend to acquire a far higher part of the increase in national income from growth than the poor (2002).

Of fact, the poor will benefit in absolute terms if distributional shares remain unchanged on average: Poverty decreases with growth, but poverty increases with recession. Although other poverty lines exhibit a similar trend, the main indicator of poverty is the percentage of persons earning less than $1 per day (using 1993 purchasing power parity exchange rates). The regression line that best matches the data is also shown in the graphic.

The line almost perfectly intersects the origin, suggesting that the average poverty reduction rate at zero growth is zero, in keeping with the pattern of average inequality change of zero. The line has a slope of 2.50 and an error of 0.30 (heteroskedasticity adjusted; $R2 = 0.44$). Since the two variables vary proportionately, this may be seen as an overall "growth elasticity" of poverty.

Accordingly, the percentage of the population living below $1 per day (at 1993 purchasing power parity) decreases on average by 2.5% with every 1% rise in the mean. For instance, a 3% rise in the mean would reduce the number of nations where precisely half of the population earns less than $1 per day to roughly 0.46. Additionally, a 3% decrease in mean income will result in an average increase in the poverty rate to 0.54. One cannot rule out the null hypothesis that the elasticity is the same in both directions since there is no evidence in the data to suggest that it differs when the mean is growing vs dropping (the t-statistic is 0.11).

Therefore, there is little evidence that distributional shifts aid in protecting the poor amid declines in the quality of life. Let's start by taking a look at distribution throughout the developing globe in the 1990s. Rising inequality in the developing world as a whole may impede overall poverty reduction in the same way that rising inequality in one nation can obviously hinder possibilities for economic progress. Has it been taking place?

According to estimates, 23% of the population in developing countries lived in households with consumption per capita less than $1 per day in

1998 (at 1993 purchasing power parity), which was only 4% less than in 1987. (*Chen and Ravallion 2001*). With around 1.2 billion people living on less than $1 per day, the overall number of the poor by this metric was about the same in 1998 as it was in 1987. *Chen and Ravallion (2001)* make an effort to determine what part the deteriorating distribution played in explaining the 1990s' underwhelming progress in reducing overall poverty.

They simulate what would have happened between 1987 and 1998 in developing and transitional countries if there had been no change in the overall interpersonal distribution. In other words, the growth rate in the (population-weighted) survey mean across their whole data set indicates that household consumption and income increase at the same pace. Thus, during the time period, the interpersonal consumption Lorenz curve from 1987 for the developing world as a whole would not change.

This distribution-neutral simulation would result in lower poverty in 1998 than was actually observed if it were true that distribution is deteriorating over time in the developing world as a whole. *Chen and Ravallion* discover that the distribution neutral case would have resulted in a poverty rate of 24.4% rather than the 23.44% estimated from the data for 1998. This suggests that, from the perspective of the poor, there was no worsening in the overall interpersonal distribution.

In fact, the measured poverty rate in 1998 is slightly lower than the simulated rate with no change in distribution, indicating that the actual distributional changes were slightly pro-poor. However, a closer examination of this finding reveals that China's economic growth is almost entirely to blame for the difference. If China is excluded from the aforementioned calculation, the simulated poverty rate in 1998 is 25.9%, which is nearly identical to the actual rate (25.2 percent, excluding China).

Accordingly, from the perspective of the poor, the overall state of income distribution has not gotten worse since the 1990s. But this overall picture conceals more than it makes clear. The gains to the poor from a particular rate of growth are heterogeneous, as was mentioned in the previous section.

Underlying this heterogeneity is the fact that, in most developing economies, inequality changes over time in both directions during periods of growth and contraction, but it typically declines at a much slower rate than in nations with more equitable growth. Among nations with rising average incomes and rising inequality, the median rate of decline in the percentage of the population living on less than $1 per day was 1.3% per year.

Diverse impacts on poverty coexist with aggregate distribution neutrality.

What is happening to inequality between the surveys?	What is happening to average household income between the surveys?	
	Falling	Rising
Rising	(16% of spell)	(30% of spell)
	Poverty is rising at a median rate of 14.3% per year	Poverty is falling at a median rate of 1.3% per year
Falling	(26% of spell)	(27% of spell)
	Poverty is rising at a median rate of 1.7% per year	Poverty is falling at a median rate of 9.6% per year

One way inequality can matter to the rate of poverty reduction is through the rate of growth in average income. In defiance of the assumption that there is a net trade-off, a variety of reasons have been presented for why more equality might actually be beneficial for development (see, for example, *Benabou 1996; Aghion, Caroli*, and *Garcia-Penalosa 1999; Bardhan, Bowles, and Gintis 1999)*. An argument that seems reasonable claims that there are flaws in the credit market that prevent individuals from taking advantage of chances to invest in (human and physical) capital that would promote growth.

For the poor, the production loss resulting from the market failure will be larger due to diminishing marginal products of capital. Therefore, the economy will expand at a slower pace the more impoverished individuals there are in it. A claim that nations with larger starting income inequality saw lower rates of growth while adjusting for other characteristics like initial average income, trade openness and the inflation rate is partially supported by cross-country comparisons of growth rates. Some researchers have questioned the reliability of this conclusion. Finding this link experimentally poses challenging issues, as the findings reported in the literature have not held up to other specifications, such as accounting for nation fixed effects (*Forbes 1997; Li and Zou 1998; Barro 2000*).

Once again, there are several issues with the data and techniques used. Both the levels and trends of measured income inequality are subject to measurement errors, which include issues with comparability between nations and over time brought on by survey error (sampling and non-sampling) and heterogeneity in survey design and processing (see, for instance, *Atkinson and Brandolini 1999*).

Since the signal-to-noise ratio for changes in measured inequality in available data sets may be fairly low, one anticipates that this will matter more to tests that account for nation fixed effects than to typical growth regressions. In the growth of inequality fixed-effects regressions, a greater attenuation bias should be anticipated. *Knowles (2001)* shows that cutting the data set to address the comparability issues affects the findings produced in significant ways. He uses a pooled regression of growth on inequality. The use of more current and similar metrics of disparity in consumer expenditures, according to Knowles, does show a considerable negative impact of inequality on growth.

Another issue is that, in light of credit market failures, erroneous inequality effects in an aggregate growth regression may result from the assumptions used in aggregating across micro-relationships. Although actual findings for China in *Ravallion (1998)* show that regional aggregation masks the detrimental impact of inequality on development, theoretically, the direction of this bias might go either way.

The popular belief that beginning inequality has a linear impact on overall development is also debatable; *Banerjee and Duflo (1999)* find evidence that increases in income disparity have a negative impact on growth regardless of the direction of the changes. It is also debatable which controls were used to determine the relationship; for instance, the human capital stock was not taken into account in previous studies of the impact of inequality on growth, despite the fact that inequality is likely to have an impact on growth by reducing investment in human capital.

Overall, the data from cross-country growth regressions seem to support the idea that inequality stunts growth more strongly than the opposing idea, which for decades predominated in development economics. That does not, however, guarantee that any decrease in inequality would increase growth; on the contrary, it may have the reverse impact if it detracts from other elements that are also proven to be important for development. The benefits of reducing inequality via increasing local or international commerce or economic distortions on growth and poverty reduction are unclear.

It is interesting to inquire as to whether there could be an alternative method of testing for an influence of initial distribution on growth given the reservations about previous studies based on cross-country averages. Returning to the numerous hypotheses on the potential importance of initial distribution, it can be shown that many of the suggested models have significant, verifiable implications for microdata. As an example, consider the fact that many theoretical models based on credit market failures have the characteristic that an individual's income or wealth at a given point in time is a rising concave function of its own historical worth.

Micro panel data can be used to test this implication of the class of distribution-dependent growth models based on credit market failures. *Lokshin and Ravallion (2001)* provide evidence in favor of this claim using panel data for Hungary and Russia, and *Jalan and Ravallion (2002)* find a similar conclusion when using panel data for China.

Finding the required non-linearity in household-level income dynamics would not support public redistribution as a strategy for promoting overall growth, similar to macro assessments of whether inequality is harmful to growth. To allow for (potentially endogenously placed) governmental programs, dynamic micro models of income or consumption may be enhanced with the proper data. Hope for a fuller comprehension of the policy consequences may lie in microstructural modeling of growth in the context of certain redistributive actions.

A high starting level of inequality might hinder opportunities for pro-poor development even when inequality is not increasing. One may anticipate that the poor will typically get a bigger proportion of the benefits from growth in an economy where inequality is low and does not increase over time than in an economy where inequality is high. If inequality tends to increase when it is low, and there is some evidence of such "inequality convergence," then this expectation will not necessarily be supported by the facts (*Benabou 1996, Ravallion 2001a,b*). Therefore, it is a question of empirical fact as to whether or not high inequality really reduces the growth elasticity of poverty. The data seems to support this. The distribution-corrected rate of increase in average income, which is equal to a measure of baseline equality (100 minus a measure of inequality) times the rate of growth, is a key factor in determining the pace of poverty reduction.

In a regression for the rate of poverty reduction, the distribution-corrected growth rate actually outperforms the standard growth rate *(Ravallion 1997)*. It is the distribution-corrected rate of growth, not the growth rate, that counts. This may be modeled as a relatively straightforward model where the distribution-corrected rate of growth is exactly proportional to the proportionate rate of change in the incidence of poverty (P) between surveys. By adding an error component, this can be stated as follows:

$$\triangle \ln P_{it} = y (1 - G_{i,t-r}) \triangle \ln Y_{it} + \varepsilon_{it},$$

Where Gi,t- is the Gini index (between zero and one) for the nation I at the start of the spell, Yit is the true value of the survey mean at date t, and is a parameter to be estimated. Where the difference is taken between surveys that are years apart (which fluctuates across countries and over time). Again, a potential issue with this estimate is that the changes in P and Y can be subject to measurement errors that are (negatively) linked. By omitting the observations for Eastern Europe and Central Asia (where the instrument fails) and using the growth rate in PCE per capita from the national accounts as the instrumental variable for the growth rate in the survey means, I found a lower estimate of, namely—2.94, with a standard error of 1.18.

With increasing levels of beginning inequality, the elasticity of poverty to growth significantly decreases. Think about a 2% annual growth rate per capita (roughly the mean for low-income countries in the 1990s). Using = 3, a nation with high inequality (let's say a Gini index of 60%) may anticipate a rate of poverty reduction of 2.4% per year. With a Gini of 30%, a nation with reasonably low inequality should anticipate a rate of poverty reduction of 4.2% annually. What particular features of inequality matter is not clear from the data above. Theoretical justifications based on credit market failures emphasize asset disparity above income inequality in terms of relevance.

There is proof that asset disparity has a negative impact on growth (see, for example, *Birdsall and Londoo 1997, Deininger and Olinto 2000*, which both used cross-country data, and *Ravallion 1998*, which used regional data for China). We can assemble a lengthy series of generally similar survey data going back to roughly 1960 for rates of poverty reduction among states in India, and these data have provided some hints. These data analysis support the idea that India's economic progress has tended to lessen poverty.

Poverty decreased as a result of increased governmental development investment, average agricultural yields, and (urban and rural) non-farm production *(Ravallion and Datt 2002)*. However, there are major regional differences in how poverty in India has changed as non-farm productivity has increased. The variations mirrored methodical variations in the starting circumstances. The likelihood of the poor contributing to the expansion of the non-farm sector was hindered by low farm output, low rural living standards in comparison to metropolitan regions, and inadequate basic education.

With a rising non-farm sector, poverty reduction and rural and human resource development tend to work in concert quite well. As we've seen, the statistics point to a weak or nonexistent relationship between global economic development and increases in inequality. The same is true for growth-promoting policy measures, for which substantial relationships with inequality have seldom ever been discovered, either positively or negatively. This is supported by Dollar and *Kraay (2002)*, who demonstrate that there is no link between shifts in inequality and markers of policy reform, such as increased openness.

If there is no change in inequality, then growth effects alone determine how the poor fare. This absence of a relationship between development and increases in inequality offers three primary reasons for caution when inferring policy implications. First, it's possible that this reform's apparent (on average) distribution-neutrality is only a result of the difficulty in measuring how inequality is changing. It should be underlined once again, for instance, that changes in survey design may still add a lot of noise to the observed changes in inequality, even if the major data set used above has been built to attempt to minimize as many of the issues as possible.

The facts also pertain to national averages. There are winners and losers at all income levels, even if overall inequality or poverty may not vary much over time. In fact, when survey data have followed the same families over time (referred to as "panel data"), it is extremely usual to uncover significant churning under the surface; *Baulch and Hoddinott (2000)* assemble evidence of this for a number of nations. Given that the changes in the data may be explained in part by observable qualities and quantifiable shocks, only a portion of this is likely due to measurement error (see, for example, Jalan and Ravallion 2000, using data for rural China).

Even while the general poverty rate may not change all that much, it is still possible to locate numerous individuals who have managed to leave poverty and others who have fallen into it.

For instance, a two percentage point rise in the poverty rate may be seen when comparing household earnings in Russia shortly after the 1998 financial crisis with those of the same families two years earlier. However, this was linked to a significant section of the population (18%) slipping into poverty while a much smaller amount (16%) emerged from it over the same time period *(Lokshin and Ravallion 2000)*. Even when the results are favorable overall, panel statistics and qualitative assessments often show welfare deficits for individual families.

While it is crucial to understand the overall balance of gains and losses, the fact that poverty is generally declining will not provide much comfort to people who are suffering. The starting circumstances differ greatly across reforming nations, which is a third reason why the modest correlations between policy reform and increases in general inequality might be misleading. This range of beginning circumstances variation makes systematic impacts easily concealable by averages. Since it contains lessons for policy, this argument merits further explanation.

Chapter 4

Growth, Distribution And Poverty Reduction

Over the 1990s, the amount of poverty in developing countries decreased steadily (*World Bank 2000a, 2001*). This development has, however, been extremely unevenly distributed. While poverty levels in certain areas and nations, notably in the least developed countries (LDCs), have stagnated or increased, other regions and countries have achieved remarkable progress. One explanation for these variations is economic growth performance, but there may also be basic variations in how well growth and distribution eliminate poverty in various groupings of nations.

There are two key goals for this investigation. First, it investigates if there is a regular correlation between the income and inequality elasticities of poverty and the amount of development, as measured by the level of consumption per capita.

It specifically examines whether variations in consumption rates and distribution affect poverty in LDCs differently from other low- and middle-income nations. Second, it looks at whether the outcomes are substantially impacted by various estimating techniques. Between known research, poverty elasticities have often differed significantly. Discrepancies coming from utilizing different data or systematic differences across estimating techniques might be the cause of the disparity or both.

Using the same data set for all three techniques, this chapter attempts to throw some light on this. The connections between poverty, income distribution, and economic development have been extensively studied in the literature. The key topics of interest in this research are the relationships between growth and poverty, inequality and poverty, and their relative relevance.

Poverty headcounts may be significantly impacted by even the smallest distributional changes. This is shown by *White and Anderson (2001)* using a simple arithmetic example. A 1% rise in their overall income would result from a 6.25 percentage point increase in the proportion of national income that goes to the lowest quintile of the population.

Therefore, a relatively little redistribution would have the same impact on poverty as increasing annual national income growth from 4% (which is the predicted growth rate of many African nations) to 8%. (which is necessary to achieve the poverty Millennium Development Goal). Changes in distribution have an even bigger impact on poverty trends when viewing consumer poverty from a wider perspective that also includes the severity and depth of poverty *(Creedy 1998; Wodon 1999)*. Growth in consumption lowers overall poverty as long as distribution remains stable. Different research has examined this to different degrees.

It is impossible to establish a priori if this discrepancy is due to research using different methodologies or different data sets. Numerous research use econometric analysis to calculate the growth elasticity of poverty. Using a first difference specification, *Ravallion and Chen (1997)* regress log poverty headcount ratios on log average consumption levels. Their sample is an early version of the household survey-based data collection on poverty that is currently accessible on the World Bank's website for monitoring poverty.

It has sixty-four episodes of poverty in forty-two transitional and emerging countries, including both episodes of rising and periods of falling income disparity. They calculate a poverty growth elasticity of 3.1 for the $1 per day poverty limit. The approach used by *Hanmer et al. (1999)* varies somewhat in that their bivariate econometric model includes distinct equations for nations with low, medium, and high inequality. The World Development Indicators (WDI) are the source of their data set, therefore there could be some overlap with Ravallion and Chen's data collection.

The poverty elasticities calculated by Hanmer et al. (1999) range between 0.5 and 1.5 for nations with Gini coefficients less than 0.4 and more than 0.5, respectively. The magnitude of the growing poverty elasticity is often reduced via multivariate econometric analysis. To capture the traits of the development route, Hanmer and Naschold (2000) use an enlarged multivariate regression model that incorporates qualitative and structural factors. The WDI is used once again to extract the data. The income poverty elasticity alone decreases to a maximum of 0.9 but the overall poverty elasticities, or the entire influence of growth and other factors on poverty, stay around 1.5.

De Janvry and Sadoulet (2000) found comparable magnitudes of poverty elasticities for a group of twelve Latin American nations by including included qualitative and structural components in their econometric model. In other research, the growth elasticity of poverty is estimated for individual nations. For 39 developing nations, *Demery, Sen, and Viswanath (1995)* distinguished the cumulative distribution function of income or consumption in the vicinity of the poverty line.

With greater values in Asia than in Africa and Latin America in between, the resultant poverty elasticities exhibit broad variability around the mean poverty elasticity of 1.89 and range from almost zero (for Zambia) to over four (for Singapore). A theoretical, identity-based technique to determine country-specific poverty elasticities from Lorenz curves has been devised by *Bourguignon (2000)*. Applying this technique to an unidentified data set, Collier and Dollar (2001) get mean and median poverty elasticities of around 2, which they then use to forecast future changes in poverty.

They contend that average elasticities determined from global cross-country studies are sufficient for establishing estimates of poverty at the global level since variations in the elasticity of poverty caused by variations (and changes) in distribution will essentially balance out. However, when we take the study below the world average level, we must confirm that we can actually utilize a single elasticity.

Since this relies on how the income distribution has changed over time and the characteristics of the chosen poverty measure, it is impossible to predict how consumption disparity would impact the consumption poverty elasticity in the abstract *(Ravallion 1997)*. The amount of the consumption poverty elasticity, however, consistently fluctuates with income or consumption disparity, according to empirical data *(Ravallion and Sen 1996; Ravallion 1997; Hanmer et al. 1999)*. This variance may be rather significant.

For instance, *Hanmer and Naschold (2000)* divide their sample of 121 observations into two categories: those with Ginis higher than 0.43 and those with Ginis lower than 0.43. They discover that in order to reduce poverty at the same pace as low inequality nations, high inequality countries require growth rates that are almost three times higher. Theoretically, *Bourguignon (2000)* and Heltberg (2003) demonstrate why the absolute value of the elasticity should rise with the amount of per capita consumption in addition to this fluctuation with the distribution. The essential premise of this connection is that any further growth will result in more individuals moving out of poverty since previous growth will have pushed the poor closer to the poverty line. *Lipton (2001)* raises two objections to this assumption.

It does so for two reasons: first, it overlooks the reality that a sizable section of the population becomes impoverished each year, and second, individuals who remained in poverty throughout previous development periods are also those who have the least chance of escaping it via future growth. However, evidence from several case studies has shown a positive correlation between average consumption and poverty elasticity of growth *(Bourguignon 2000)*. Therefore, allowing for various elasticities across income categories makes logical.

According to conventional opinion, inequality trends are stable, hence nothing can be done to change the distribution of wealth *(Deininger and Squire 1996; Li, Squire, and Zou 1998)*. As a result, distribution was sometimes overlooked while examining how growth and poverty relate to one another. Where it existed, it is usually found that the growth effect outweighs the impact of changes in distribution on poverty. Although generally speaking, this is not true for all nations and situations. When *White and Anderson (2001)* break down increases in the lowest income quintile's income into growth and distribution impacts, they find that, for one-fourth of the 143 growth episodes they examined, the inequality effect was bigger than the growth effect.

Hanmer and Naschold's (2000) simulations of development and distribution scenarios demonstrate how, in the event of extremely unequal nations, the inequality impact might outweigh the growth benefit, especially in underdeveloped areas with slow historical growth rates like sub-Saharan Africa. The majority of empirical studies that look at the connection between changes in distribution, consumption growth, and poverty reduction rely on one of three methodologies: either estimating consumption and distribution elasticities through econometric analysis, or computing them at a specific point on the cumulative consumption distribution function, or deriving arithmetic relationships from poverty spells between two household surveys.

All three are used in this research, first to see whether the methodological choice affected the findings and then to forecast the range of poverty levels in 2015. The same data collection is used by all techniques, notably the World Bank's poverty monitoring website's data on poverty and distribution66, which is based on information gathered by *Chen and Ravallion (2000)*. The 162 surveys in the sample, which encompass 60 countries and around 75 percent of the world's population in developing nations, were conducted between 1980 and 1998. (see table below).

Surveys for Eastern Europe and Central Asia are not included in the data collection because of the region's extreme recent developments in poverty and inequality, as well as the varying quality of the data (see, e.g. Mosley and Kalyuzhnova 2000; Luttmer 2001).

	Total number of surveys in sample	Total number of countries in sample	Population covered by at least one survey (%)	Population in income group (in millions)
All developing countries	162	60	76	5006
LCDs	31	18	56	614
Other low income	50	13	94	2917
Middle income	84	29	51	1475

Instead of focusing on money, poverty is measured by consumption. The headcount index displays the proportion of people who live on less than $1.08 per day (PPP) in 1993. Due to its availability for the largest number of nations, the Gini coefficient is employed as a summary indicator of the national income distribution. It is vital to keep in mind the inherent limitations of the data before moving on to the analysis and interpretation of the findings.

Some household surveys assess consumption, while others measure income, and international comparability is hampered by challenges in measuring buying power parities between nations and across time. Survey and pricing data might also be out-of-date. Additionally, there isn't much of an alternative to employing cross-country methodologies to evaluate what are fundamentally country-specific processes due to the restricted availability of data for particular nations. However, as polls are now more accurate and comprehensive, overall findings should be more dependable than in the past *(World Bank 2000b)*.

Sensitivity experiments verified that the choice of the poverty line affects consumption poverty elasticities. The poverty elasticities are reduced by between 16 and 63 percent when the poverty line is raised by 10%69, with the percentage variance being greater the higher the average income. For the purpose of reducing poverty, consumption distribution is important.

The relationship between the amount of development and the magnitude of the inequality regression coefficient, in contrast to consumption, is not very clear. Other low-income nations' inequality elasticity is somewhat lower than that of LDCs. Calculating point elasticities using the cumulative distribution of per capita consumption from individual household surveys is another way to determine how changes in income distribution and consumption growth may affect poverty. By differentiating the cumulative distribution function in the vicinity of the poverty line, this is accomplished. Using the POVCAL program, estimates of consumption and inequality poverty elasticities were created *(Datt, Chen, and Ravallion 1993)*. The elasticities are based on each nation's most recent household survey.

While the Gini elasticities assume constant mean income, the consumption growth elasticities of poverty imply distributional neutral growth. The median elasticities for developing nations as a whole, as well as for the three income categories, are summarized in the following table. For all emerging nations, the consumption growth elasticity concerning headcount (H_0) is 1.57. Once again, estimates for other low- and middle-income nations are close together at around 1.7, with LDCs having by far the lowest consumer poverty elasticities (0.91) of any low- and middle-income country.

Sub-Saharan Africa has the lowest elasticities, while East Asia Pacific and South Asia have the highest elasticities, with the other regions falling somewhere in between. This pattern is seen when the estimates of poverty consumption elasticities by region are combined *(Demery, Sen, and Viswanath 1995)*. The predicted positive sign is seen for all of the Gini elasticities.

As income distribution grows increasingly uneven, poverty rises. The third method of determining poverty consumption elasticities is to arithmetically compute them from the poverty spells. This method also increases the Gini elasticities. Two comparable surveys for a specific nation at two different times, carried out using comparable procedures, constitute a poverty spell (e.g. consumption or income surveys).

The spells study is based on 102 spells in all, including 15 spells for LDCs, 36 for other low-income countries, and 51 for middle-income nations. By dividing the log change in mean consumption by the log change in headcounts from LDCs to middle-income nations, poverty elasticities were calculated for each nation.

	Econometric model	POVCAL	Poverty spells
All developing countries	-1.68	-1.57	-1.48
LDCc	-0.61	-0.91	-0.82
Other low income	-2.07	-1.63	-1.61
Middle income	-1.96	-1.74	-1.60

How comparable the elasticities are when comparing the findings from the three techniques is instantly apparent. There are three key findings. First, compared to other emerging nations, LDCs have substantially lower poverty elasticity rates. This empirical finding supports what theory predicts (*Bourguignon 2000; Heltberg*, this volume): there is a systematic correlation between the degree of development and the ability of growth to reduce poverty.

Growth's efficacy in eradicating poverty may vary across LDCs and other developing nations much more than the findings show. This is because many LDCs had periods of negative growth over the years included in the data set and the poverty elasticity of consumption growth is, if anything, greater during times of recession than during ensuing recoveries (*Cornia 1994*). The results also suggest a significant geographical disparity between sub-

Saharan Africa and other parts of the globe since fifteen of the eighteen LDCs in the sample are from this continent.

Second, although inequality is important for reducing poverty, there is no clear correlation between inequality's significance and development status. The inequality impact on poverty is unavoidably greater relative to the growth effect than in other developing nations due to the low poverty consumption elasticities in LDCs. Third, the findings are unaffected by the approach chosen.

Therefore, it is highly probable that utilizing various data sets led to different conclusions in earlier investigations. However, just comparing consumption elasticities with distribution elasticities of poverty makes it impossible to draw any significant conclusions. To estimate the effects of changes in consumption and distribution for a variety of realistic growth and inequality scenarios is the primary goal of the poverty forecasts in this section. Of course, the forecasts also provide separate "numbers" for the number of people living in poverty in 2015.

The discussion in this part concentrates more on the various projection patterns that emerge between the three income categories and between different projection scenarios rather than the precise headcounts expected for 2015 since they are susceptible to numerous uncertainties. The conclusions of the poverty projections are simple extrapolations that start with the most recent headcount ratios.

Estimates are provided for six scenarios, which combine two possibilities for consumption growth with three scenarios for distribution. The regional consumption per capita predictions from the Global Economic Prospects 2001 are used in the situation with a greater rate of consumption growth. The base scenario implies that future regional consumption growth will be similar to that in the 1990s. The consumption projections for each income group in all scenarios are created using the weighted average of the areas within each income group.

The three distribution scenarios involve a steady pattern of distribution, linear growth or decrease in the Gini coefficient by the same percentage point over a period of 15 years until 2015. Although the Gini's rate of change is rather arbitrary, it does have some foundation in research on Gini trends. For instance, using the typical Deininger and Squire data set, *Deininger and Squire (1996)* estimate a 0.28 percent average yearly shift in Gini coefficients.

This yearly change is about doubled by the five percentage point change. The doubling of the rate might be seen as a promise to shift the income distribution as the Deininger and Squire finding represents completely arbitrary fluctuations in Gini. This may seem too ambitious to some, but we should also keep in mind that previous distribution adjustments happened without active policy involvement since research and development policy had a growth-focused approach rather than a distribution-focused one.

Perhaps more can be accomplished in the future if distribution difficulties are given more focus. Additionally, bigger shifts are not wholly speculative; we do not need to turn to the transition economies to uncover distributional changes that are more significant than the possibilities presented here and took place over shorter times. For instance, according to *Ali and Thorbecke (2000)*, inequality rose in sub-Saharan Africa during the 1970s and declined in Latin America during the 1980s (*Birdsall, Pinckney, and Sabot 1996*).

Ranges represent the predictions. These demonstrate the variation in outcomes across the various techniques. In any case, it is better to use ranges for something as speculative as long-term estimates. Growth's ability to eradicate poverty is influenced by the degree of development as measured by per capita consumption. The elasticities of consumption growth in LDCs are only between a third and half as large as those in other emerging nations. Growth has therefore had a far less positive impact on the impoverished in LDCs.

Over the last 20 years, this has worsened the impact of slow development and led to static or increasing poverty levels in this group of nations. The findings of the many approaches used to evaluate the growth-poverty link using the same data have been relatively comparable, indicating that the conclusions are not considerably impacted by the methodology used. Therefore, rather than different approaches, it is most probable that different results in earlier research were obtained by utilizing different data sets.

The value of consumption disparity for reducing poverty and the degree of development are not systematically related. However, since LDCs have low poverty consumption elasticities compared to other developing nations, the impact of inequality on poverty is greater than that of growth. According to the econometric findings, the distribution impact can be just as potent as the consumption effect. How far we can interpret these findings is constrained by two significant considerations.

First, simulations make the assumption that the associations being studied by the regression analysis will continue to exist in the future. Of course, things might change in the future. Indeed, breaking old bonds in LDCs is one of the major obstacles. Second, data from cross-country analysis are used to calculate national averages. Averages, however, are just that. While some nations may be considered "average," most cannot.

We must be very cautious when interpreting the findings at the national level due to the inherent limitations of cross-country research. The forecasts for poverty show that the number of people living on less than $1.08 a day is predicted to decline, and developing nations as a whole are likely to accomplish the Millennium Development Goal of halving poverty by 2015. Although it was intended to be a worldwide goal, halving poverty should likely also apply to specific subgroups and nations.

However, many of the poorest nations won't achieve the goal due to the stark variations in wealth across populations. The tendency that LDCs are likely to lag behind other emerging nations is especially concerning. In the best-case scenario, the number of poor people in LDCs remains unchanged; in the worst-case scenario, poverty incidence will considerably rise. While increases in consumption per capita are arguably the most crucial factor in eliminating poverty in other low- and middle-income nations, distributional impacts might be just as significant in LDCs.

For this group of nations to achieve any real headway toward the MDGs, consumption growth and distribution reform must be combined. We shouldn't take the precise amounts of anticipated poverty too seriously because of the disclaimers that apply to the study that is given here. The simulations, however, make it evident that the patterns of probable poverty growth in LDCs and other emerging nations follow quite different tendencies. What do the results signify in terms of policy?

The key takeaway from this chapter may be that changes in distribution are important for reducing poverty in LDCs, and this is especially true when considering measures of poverty's depth and severity, which are more sensitive to the distribution of income. Even if we were to reject all of the conclusions in this chapter and insist that growth is always the key to eradicating poverty, we should still focus more on distribution since greater inequality has been shown to inhibit economic progress.

Each of these justifications alone shows that we should focus on distribution difficulties if we are serious about eradicating poverty, particularly in the world's poorest nations. They provide a strong argument for placing distribution at the center of efforts to reduce poverty when taken together. How should this affect actual policy? Although cross-country study has recognized inequality as a crucial component of reducing poverty, it offers little guidance on how to address the issue. We still don't fully understand the factors that impact inequality levels. To better understand what causes changes in distribution and which of these characteristics policies may and should address, further research at the national level is required. Country case studies may also assist us in comprehending why development in LDCs has a less significant influence on eradicating poverty.

The analysis in this study, as in many others, is restricted to a consumption-based perspective on inequality and poverty. Nowadays, it is commonly acknowledged that poverty has several dimensions, both in theory and policy as well as in research. The drivers of inequality's non-income dimensions, on the other hand, are still predominantly examined in relation to its income dimension, leaving room for more study in this field.

Chapter 5

Geographic Profile Of Profit: Evidence From Three Developing Countries

The geographical distribution of poverty is described in depth through poverty maps. Governments, non-governmental organizations, and international institutions who wish to increase the effect that their expenditure has on the impoverished may find these to be of great use. For instance, as a first step in helping the poor, many developing nations utilize poverty maps to direct the allocation of resources among local governments or organizations.

Poverty maps may be a useful research tool as well. Distributions of income and wealth have once again assumed a key role in growth and development theories as a result of recent theoretical advancements. Individual health or levels of violence are only two examples of the particular socio-economic outcomes that distributions of well-being are thought to influence. However, due to the low quality of distributional data, the development of comprehensive regional poverty profiles and empirical assessment of the significance of theoretical linkages have been hampered.

In-depth household surveys with appropriate income and consumption measurements are samples, and as a result, they are seldom representative or large enough at low levels of disaggregation to provide statistically valid results. The three developing nations under examination here can only be divided into areas with hundreds of thousands of homes using sample data. While this is going on, income and consumption are either completely absent from census statistics (or big sample data) that are large enough to enable disaggregation, or they are measured inaccurately.

This chapter provides a short description of a newly developed statistical method for combining data sources in order to benefit from the wide coverage of a census and the precise information available in home sample surveys (*Elbers, Lanjouw, and Lanjouw 2002*).

We estimate (rather than directly measure) poverty and inequality at a disaggregated level based on a household per capita measure of spending, y, using a household survey to impute missing information from the census. The concept is easy to understand. First, a model of y is generated using sample survey data while limiting the explanatory variables to those that are either shared by the survey and census or variables from a tertiary data set that can be connected to both of those data sets.

Then, using parameter estimates from the "first stage" model of y, we estimate the predicted level of W given the census-based observable features of the population of interest, using W to represent an indication of poverty or inequality. A similar strategy might be used for other household well-being indicators including assets, income, or employment. New research employing data from Brazil expands the strategy to replace the whole unit record level census with a thorough but small sample survey and a much bigger sample survey data collection (*Elbers, Lanjouw, and Lanjouw 2002*).

Using data from Ecuador, Madagascar, and South Africa as examples, we show that the technique produces accurate estimates of poverty at a highly disaggregated level. For example, the 95% confidence intervals on our estimates of poverty headcount rates for "counties" of around 1000–2000 families are about the same size as the intervals on the estimates at the stratum (region) level in the household surveys.

These final ones often have millions of residences and have populations far over 100,000. Policymakers and academics may test a wide range of hypotheses at levels of disaggregation where assumptions about stable underlying structures are more tenable than at a cross-country level thanks to excellent welfare estimates for groups the size of towns, villages, or even neighborhoods. The strategy will likely be beneficial in a variety of circumstances given that it functions adequately in three environments that are as diverse as the nations described in this chapter.

Prior to applying the parameter estimates to the census data to produce poverty statistics, the survey data are used to construct a prediction model for consumption. Therefore, one of the main premises is that the models generated using survey data also hold true for census observations. This makes the most sense if the survey and census years are the same. In this situation, straightforward checks may be made by contrasting the estimates with the sample data's fundamental statistics on inequality or poverty.

The welfare estimates derived correspond to the census year, whose explanatory factors serve as the foundation for the expected spending distribution if alternative years are utilized but the assumption is deemed plausible. The clear acknowledgment that poverty or inequality statistics computed using an income or consumption model are statistically unreliable is a key component of the methodology used here. Calculating standard errors is necessary. Brief summaries of *Elbers, Lanjouw, and Lanjouw's* debate may be found in the subsections below (2002).

Per-capita household expenditure, y$_h$, is related to a set of observable characteristics, x$_h$:

$$\ln y_h = E[\ln y_h | x_h] + u_h$$

Using a linear approximation, we model the observed log per capita expenditure for household *h* as

$$\ln y_h = x_h^T \beta + u_h,$$

*where β is a vector of parameters and uh is a disturbance term satisfying E[uh|**x**h] = 0. In applications we allow for location effects and heteroskedasticity in the distribution of the disturbances.*

Utilizing data from the household survey, the eqn above was calculated. We're interested in utilizing these estimations to determine the well-being of a region or population for whom we don't have enough data on expenditures or none at all. We refer to our target population as a "county" even though the disaggregation may be along any dimension, not just geographic. There are mh family members in household h.

Although the home serves as the unit of observation for expenditures, we are more often interested in welfare indicators based on individuals. As a result, we create the formula W (m,X,u), where m is a vector of household sizes, X is a matrix of observable qualities, and u is a vector of disturbances. Data from the household survey and unit record census were pooled in all three of the nations under consideration.

The poverty map for Ecuador is based on household survey data from 1994 and census data from 1990, both of which were gathered by INEC, the National Statistical Institute of Ecuador. About 2 million households were included in the census. The sample survey (Encuesta de Condiciones de

Vida, ECV) is based on the methodology of the World Bank's Living Standards Measurement Surveys and includes little under 4500 homes. The survey offers thorough data on a variety of subjects, including food consumption, non-food consumption, labor activities, agricultural practices, entrepreneurial activities, and access to services like education and health.

The three major agroclimatic zones in the nation and a breakdown of rural and urban areas are used to cluster and stratify the survey. Additionally, Quito and Guayaquil, Ecuador's two largest cities, are oversampled. Using a Laspeyres food price index and accounting for geographic price fluctuation, Hentschel and Lanjouw (1996) create a household consumption aggregate that reflects the spending habits of the underprivileged.

The poverty figures shown here are based on the World Bank's consumption poverty level of 45,476 sucres per person per fortnight, or around $1.50 per person per day. Despite the fact that the 1994 ECV data were gathered four years after the census, we continue to operate on the presumption that the 1994 consumption model is acceptable for 1990. Ecuador had a period of relative stability between 1990 and 1994. The assumption of minimal change during the period is supported by comparative summary statistics on a number of common variables from the two data sets.

Hentschel et al. go into further detail about this data and the implementation of poverty mapping in Ecuador (2000). The estimates of poverty at the local level in Madagascar were derived from three data sources. the Direction de la Démographie et Statistique Social (DDSS) of the Institut National de la Statistique's 1993 unit record population census data (INSTAT).

Second, the Direction des Statistique des Ménages (DSM) of INSTAT conducted the Enquête Permanente Auprès des Ménages (EPM), a household survey, among about 4508 families between May 1993 and April 1994. Thirdly, we used various geographical and environmental results at the fivondrona level (such as portraying a group of "firaisanas" or communes). 101 An imputed stream of consumption from the possession of consumer durables is one of the components of the welfare indicator that supports the poverty map of Madagascar. In Mistiaen et al., further information is given (2002). The South African poverty map was similarly produced using the combination of three data sources. The OHS (October Household Study), a yearly survey that focuses on certain important indicators of living patterns in South Africa, is the first.

It focuses on vital statistics, housing, access to services, individual education, internal migration, employment, and housing. 29,700 homes were questioned as part of the survey's 1995 round. The source of data on family income and spending is the Income and Expenditure Survey (IES). It was designed to work with the OHS. 28,710 homes in total were still included in the combined data set.

The 1996 population census, the third source of data, has information on nearly 8.3 million homes. In a way similar to the OHS, it gathered data on household composition as well as certain specifics on housing and services. Alderman et al. provide further information (2002). The home sample survey is used to conduct the first estimate. The household survey is divided into a number of areas and is representative at that level for each of the three nations that are discussed in this chapter.

There are one or more layers of clustering within each area. Households are chosen at random from a census enumeration area at the top level. These groupings are referred to as "clusters" and are indicated by the letter "c." Regional totals may be calculated thanks to expansion factors.

The creation of a precise empirical model of home consumption is our top priority. Think about the following model:

$$Iny_{ch} = E\left[Iny_{ch}|x_{ch}^T\right] + u_{ch} = x_{ch}\beta + \eta_c + \varepsilon_{ch},$$

where η and ε are independent of each other and uncorrelated with observables. This specification permits the disturbances' intra-cluster correlation.

Location is expected to affect household income and consumption, and even with a large number of regressors, part of the influence of location may still be unaccounted for. There are diminishing returns from aggregating across more homes for any given disturbance variance, σ^2_{ch}, as the proportion of that variation that is attributable to the common component, c, increases.

Estimates of welfare grow less accurate. Furthermore, underestimating the standard errors on poverty estimates would arise from neglecting to take geographic correlation in the disturbances into account. Since unexplained location effects impair the accuracy of poverty estimations, the initial objective is to choose and create explanatory variables that will enable as much as possible variation in consumption owing to geography. We take four approaches to this.

i. We estimate different models for each stratum in the country's respective survey.

ii. We include in our specification household-level indicators of connection to various networked infrastructure services, such as electricity, piped water, networked waste disposal, telephone, etc. To the extent that all or most households within a given neighbourhood or community are likely to enjoy similar levels of access to such networked infrastructure, these variables might capture unobserved location effects.

iii. Third, we calculate means at the enumeration area (EA) level in the census (generally corresponding to the 'cluster' in the household survey) of household-level variables, such as the average level of education of household heads. We then merge these EA means into the household survey and consider them for inclusion in the first stage regression specification.

iv. Finally, in the case of Madagascar we have merged a *fivondrona*-level data set provided by CARE and also consider the spatially referenced environmental variables contained in that data set for inclusion in our household expenditure models.

The following tables present stratum-level estimates of the poverty headcount in our three countries. The first illustrates that estimates of the incidence of poverty in Ecuador at the stratum-level are reasonably close to those from the census. Except for Guayaquil and Rural Sierra, the pairs of poverty estimates are statistically indistinguishable at better than a 5 per cent level of significance and are close to coinciding in several instances. The differences in estimates for
Guayaquil and Rural Sierra can reasonably be traced to changes between the 1990 census and the 1994 household survey in the exogenous variables underpinning the consumption regressions.

Stratum-level poverty rates in Ecuador (headcount)

Stratum	Household Survey (s.e.)	Census (s.e.)
Rural Costa	0.50 (0.042)	0.501 (0.024)
Urban Costa	0.25 (0.03)	0.258 (0.015)
Guayaquil	0.29 (0.027)	0.380 (0.019)
Rural Sierra	0.43 (0.027)	0.527 (0.019)
Urban Sierra	0.19 (0.026)	0.211 (0.027)
Quito	0.25 (0.033)	0.223 (0.022)
Rural Oriente	0.67 (0.054)	0.590 (0.025)
Urban Oriente	0.20 (0.05)	0.189 (0.021)

Stratum-level poverty rates in Madagascar (headcount)

Stratum	Household Survey (s.e.)	Census (s.e.)
Antananariwo Urban	0.544 (0.048)	0.462 (0.015)
Antananariwo Rural	0.767 (0.037)	0.738 (0.019)
Fianarantsoa Urban	0.674 (0.059)	0.646 (0.027)
Fianarantsoa Rural	0.769 (0.049)	0.820 (0.025)
Taomasina Urban	0.599 (0.086)	0.599 (0.018)
Taomasina Rural	0.810 (0.035)	0.786 (0.026)
Mahajanga Urban	0.329 (0.072)	0.378 (0.028)
Mahajanga Rural	0.681 (0.065)	0.695 (0.039)
Toliara Urban	0.715 (0.086)	0.713 (0.036)
Toilara Rural	0.817 (0.042)	0.800 (0.031)
Antsiranana Urban	0.473 (0.087)	0.344 (0.031)
Antsiranana Rural	0.613 (0.073)	0.581 (0.046)

Stratum-level poverty rates in South Africa (headcount)

Stratum	Household Survey (s.e.)	Census (s.e.)
Western Cape	0.12 (0.011)	0.11 (0.006)
Eastern Cape	0.45 (0.014)	0.40 (0.009)
Northern Cape	0.38 (0.030)	0.35 (0.014)
Free State	0.51 (0.022)	0.53 (0.010)
Kwazulu-Natal	0.24 (0.014)	0.25 (0.008)
Northwest Province	0.37 (0.024)	0.41 (0.011)
Mpumalanga	0.26 (0.022)	0.22 (0.011)
Northern Province	0.36 (0.021)	0.35 (0.015)

The sample and census statistics for Madagascar apply to the same time frame. The primary cause of worry in this nation is the high standard errors of the sample-based estimations. Additionally, the first stage regressions' explanatory power is only somewhat strong in one or two of the strata (an adjusted R2 of 0.24 for rural Antsiranana is the lowest obtained in any of our models).

Our forecasted poverty estimates at the census level are thus subject to quite substantial standard errors. It is challenging to argue against the equality of point estimates given the mistakes taken as a whole. The census and survey point estimates, however, are relatively close for all strata. Results from South Africa are likewise good. Point estimates from the two sources of data are quite similar at the stratum level, thus once again we are unable to rule out equality at the 5% level of significance.

Despite a sample size that is several times bigger than the average LSMS-style home survey, stratum-level standard errors in the IES survey are not minimal. These tables may be used to prove three things. First off, our estimates often closely match household survey-based estimates in all three of the nations we've looked at and are statistically indistinguishable from them. Second, the survey-based estimates' accuracy isn't all that good.

Third, our estimators' standard errors at the stratum level are consistently smaller than those found using only household survey data. This suggests that when obtaining poverty estimates in the population census, mistakes incurred by using the statistical approach described above are more than compensated by the reduction of sampling error. Next, we'll demonstrate how, without incurring any extra cost in terms of statistical accuracy, estimates of poverty may be generated using census data at degrees of disaggregation substantially below those made achievable by household survey data alone. In South Africa, the situation is quite different.

When comparing point estimates to standard errors at the police-station level, which has an average of 7500 households, the ratio is much higher than it is for the household survey at the strata level. Going to police stations would cost money in terms of the accuracy of the statistics used to determine poverty. The cost is reasonable when broken down to the level of the Magisterial Districts, of which there are 354 in South Africa and an average of 20,000 families in each.

However, it is significant to highlight that the South African IES survey's stratum-level estimations are impressively accurate due to the survey's enormous sample size (nearly 30,000 households). Even police station estimates of poverty would be seen as acceptable in South Africa if one were to use the same criteria of acceptability that are often applied to situations where LSMS-style surveys are the main source of information.

Poverty reduction is the primary objective of development initiatives, and it may be achieved via either economic expansion or income redistribution. This chapter offers a limited assessment of current research on the connections between poverty, income inequality, and economic development. The impact of economic policy on these three components is also covered. Development is a controversial idea that has important philosophical ramifications.

Our main focus is on how the three aspects of economic welfare—per capita income, income distribution, and poverty—change over time. The primary distinction between income-consumption poverty metrics and the others in terms of poverty is this. It has been suggested that a sole emphasis on income and expenses ignores crucial well-being factors that the impoverished value highly. Although all scholars agree that poverty should be seen as a multifaceted phenomenon, income poverty metrics are defended on the grounds that money is a way of meeting other requirements.

However, it may be argued that rather than using an input indicator like income, poverty should be assessed using output indicators like infant mortality, literacy rates, and enrollment rates. One may argue that many social indicators have a distributional component and may improve without necessarily suggesting an increase in the well-being of the poorest people in order to counter this point of view.

While supporters of the various approaches have previously individually made their case, there has been a move towards more agreement, and there have even been efforts to integrate the approaches in order to measure poverty. When comparing the various ideas, it can be shown that certain signs may be associated while others are not. There have sometimes been discrepancies in poverty patterns observed when quantitative analysis and participatory research are contrasted (Narayan et al. 2000). A larger definition of poverty may not affect the overall number of poor people, but it does increase the range of measures that are taken into consideration to reduce poverty *(Kanbur and Squire 1999)*. Any conversation about how economic policies and changes affect the poor always includes some discussion of income or consumption. Since household income (consumption) and the gross domestic product (GDP) are both evaluated in monetary terms, poverty indicators based on income (consumption) will be a suitable place to start when analyzing poverty.

www.ingramcontent.com/pod-product-compliance
Lightning Source LLC
Chambersburg PA
CBHW050009230526
45465CB00003BB/1326